Fl

THE NEW
AMERICAN QUILT

Lark Communications
Asheville, North Carolina

Cover:
VIRGINIA JACOBS

Sky Quilt #1
48 by 48 inches
1981

Machine pieced and quilted nylon.
Photo by Tom Bernard.

*I have been working for the past
year with machine pieced and
quilted works made of nylon flag
bunting. The kite form occurred
to me when I hung a square
sample up by one corner, and
realized that if I added a tail, I'd
have a kite!*

ISBN - 0-937274-02-X
Library of Congress Catalog Card No.: 81-66909

Copyright ©1981 by Fiberarts/Lark Books, a division of Lark Communications Corp.

Published in 1981 by:
Lark Communications Corp.
P.O. Box 2775
Asheville, North Carolina 28801

INTRODUCTION

The ancient craft of quilting may have originated as a practical measure—a technique for binding straw and cloth into a mattress—but it wasn't long before quilters began adding personal signatures to their work by creating designs with their stitching. Centuries-old quilted bedcovers are the legacies of those who couldn't resist the temptation to express their own creativity while performing an otherwise tedious and mundane task.

That creative expression has taken on more and more significance as the practical need for hand quilting has diminished. Today, quilts are often designed for purely decorative purposes, as wall hangings or fabric paintings. Galleries across the country are now catering to buyers who collect quilts, both antique and modern.

THE NEW AMERICAN QUILT covers the spectrum of contemporary quilting, from functional bedcoverings to wall quilts, from calico prints to quilted handmade paper.

All of these works have been exhibited by Quilt National, the brainchild of Ohio resident and quilter Nancy Crow. It is America's only juried competition for contemporary quilters.

"I am one of many quilters who are turning away from using the traditional quilting patterns. We are concerned with original design, and expanding the boundaries of quilting in terms of techniques and materials used. However, the only place we had to show our work was mixed-media fiber shows, where our work was displayed along with weavings, fiber sculpture or traditional quilts which followed the time-honored patchwork patterns. I felt we needed a forum which was solely devoted to contemporary quilting."

Nancy's idea coincided with the completion of a massive renovation project in Athens, Ohio, which turned a 67-year-old dairy barn into a center for cultural events. The spacious barn seemed to provide a perfect backdrop for a quilting exhibition, and in the summer of 1979 it was the home of the first Quilt National exhibition.

That event provided the platform needed to demonstrate the transformations taking place in the world of quilting. Many of the works held fast to the traditional methods of piecing and patching, but incorporated totally new concepts of design and color.

Others were the product of new techniques such as silk-screening, block printing and Xerox transfer onto fabric or handmade paper.

Such a collection of works carries the definition of quilting far beyond its traditional parameters, reflecting the changing role of this technique in contemporary crafts.

This evolution presents a challenge to jurors of such a competition. These individuals are responsible for selecting from hundreds of quilts submitted for consideration, a limited number of works which represent current trends. The jurors for Quilt National 1981— Diane Itter, fiber artist; Nancy Crow, quilter; and Daniel Butts, director of the Mansfield Art Center in Ohio—reflected on that challenge after the selection process was completed.

"I felt that in jurying the show we had a responsibility to make some sort of statement about quilts—a new definition. Even though the selection would, no doubt, reflect our personal aesthetics, we were dealing with far broader concerns . . . the quilt as an art object."

Diane Itter

"In comparing the 1981 quilts to earlier ones, I found that the artists were demonstrating a serious commitment to growth and development in their work. The quilts displayed multiple levels of sophistication and indicated a strong personal sense of direction . . . a positive growth in terms of contemporary quiltmaking."

Nancy Crow

" Many of the really exciting works of art exhibited today seem to utilize media and techniques that have been historically labeled as crafts.

A fine quilt is the epitome of the perfect blending of the craftsman's hand and the artist's eye . . . a combination that is demolishing the arbitrary distinctions between art and craft. Quilting is a growing art form which is continually changing and re-defining itself with each new quilt that comes off the frame. "

H. Daniel Butts, III

THE NEW AMERICAN QUILT reflects the state of the art in terms of contemporary quilting. It is our contribution to the family-tree of this craft. It will serve as a reference point for those who are intrigued by the history of quilting, and provide inspiration to artists who have taken on the challenge of expanding the traditional boundaries of this technique.

Lark Communications and Quilt National 1981

NOTE: With each quilt in this volume, you will find:

Name of the Designer/Artist
Title of the Work
Dimensions
Year of exhibition by Quilt National
Descriptions of methods and materials
Comments by the artist about the work

JUDY MATHIESON

Floating City
62 by 67 inches
1981

*While I was working on this quilt,
I was often called outside by the
honking of thousands of
Canadian geese flying south for
the winter. The shadows of the
four birds in "Floating City" are a
reflection of that experience.*

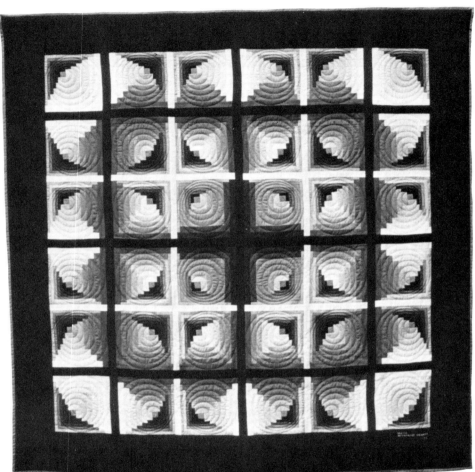

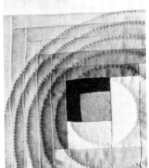

MARIA MCCORMICK-SNYDER

Log Cabin Variation
73 by 73 inches
1979

Machine pieced and hand quilted cotton.

In this piece I employed soft gradations of color to give a pulsating sense of light and perspective.

JUDI WARREN
Art Deco: Making Z's
72 by 72 inches
1981
Cotton. Photo by John Kluesener.

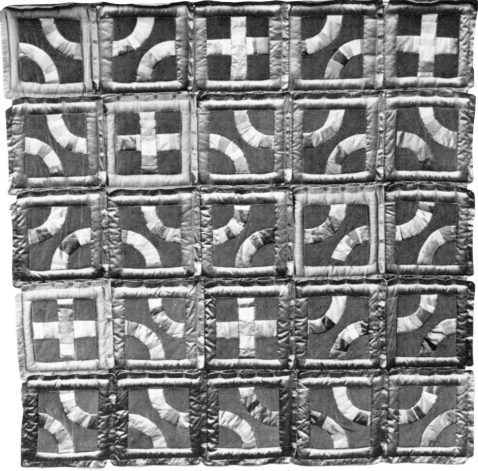

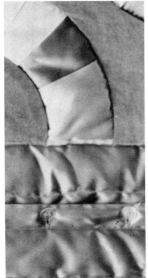

JOYCE MARQUESS

Puzzle Quilt
84 by 84 inches
1979

Satin and velveteen. Quilt can be
buttoned in any number of
arrangements.

RUTH SMILER

Matrix II
64 by 64 inches
1981

Pieced quilt.

Textural ambiguity and three-dimensional illusion are recurring design themes in my work. In "Matrix II", the bold black/white pattern is juxtaposed with colored diagonals, to create a visual illusion that suggests superimposed grids or lattices.

PRISCILLA VINCIL

Barred Fantasy
62 by 62 inches
1981

Satin ribbon and broadcloth.

NANCY HALPERN

Hilltown
71 by 73 inches
1981

Cottons and cotton blends.
Machine pieced and hand quilted.

Hilltown is my attempt to create a sense of place, a humanized landscape that is also a portable, wrappable environment. Although the original idea for this quilt came from a snowy Monet painting, I think of my town as one where the snow has been falling and has stopped just five minutes ago.

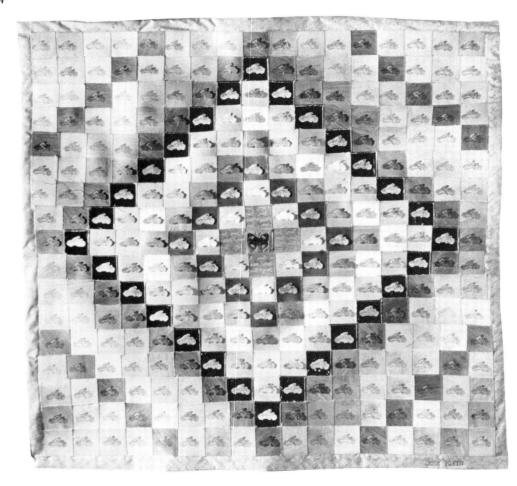

JODY KLEIN

Quilt for Outstanding
Homunculus Motorcyle Riders
35 by 35 inches
1981

Paper, fabric and laminated mylar.
Printed, drawn, stitched, stamped.

*I like my work to present a strong
graphic statement at first glance,
and also suggest mysteries to*
*those who take a closer look. The
image for this quilt is based on my
collection of antique motorcycle-
rider toys. My fantasy is that this
rider is on a gentle journey to no
place in particular.*

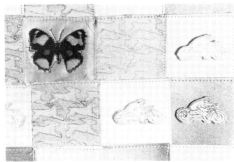

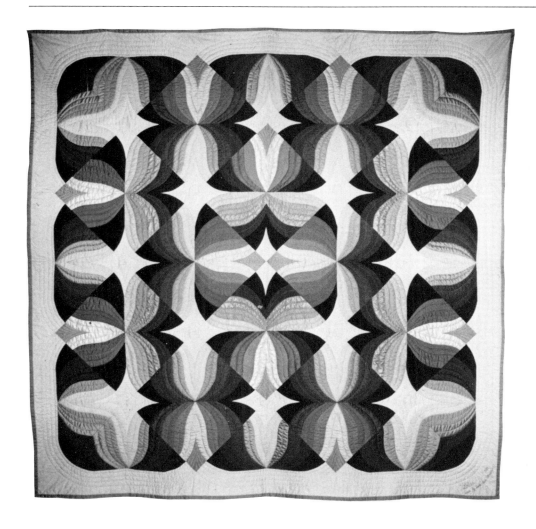

DORLE STERN-STRAETER

Lotus
84 by 84 inches
1981

Machine pieced and hand quilted
cotton.

SUSAN SCHROEDER
#2
75 by 48 inches
1981

Pieced batik.

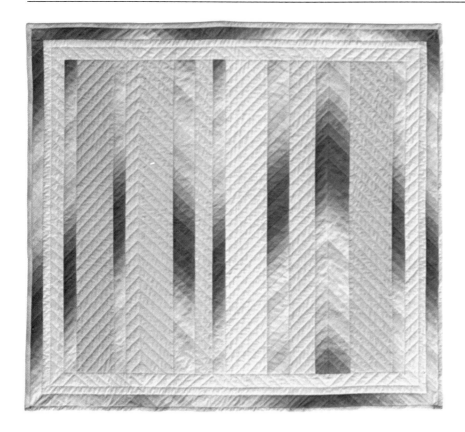

JAN MYERS

Beulahland
42 by 46 inches
1981

Hand dyed cotton muslin.
Machine pieced.

*By dyeing all of my own fabrics, I
can achieve subtle gradations
from light to dark or hue to hue. I
am fascinated with color and
light, and I aim for color and
value placement that will give
each work its own light.*

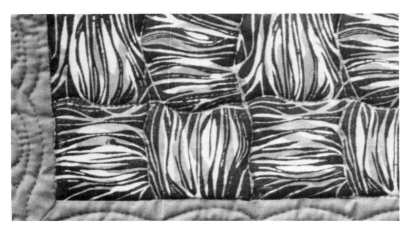

ANN RANKIN

Batik, Block and
Screen Printed Quilt
91 by 105 inches
1979

White cotton sateen. Batiked,
screen printed, block printed and
hand quilted.

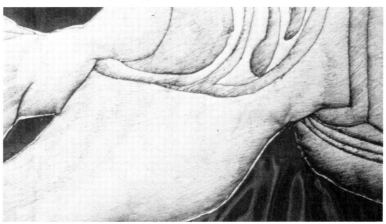

CYNTHIA NIXON-HUDSON

Melinda's Window
48 by 60 inches
1981

Trapunto, applique and machine
quilting. Ink-drawn passages.

JUDITH DINGLE

Windows
80 by 84 inches
1981

Cottons and cotton blends.

PAUL WESLEY WALKER

Stairway to Heaven
80 by 88 inches
1981

Cotton. Hand pieced and hand quilted.

Visualizing my image for this quilt was a special moment . . . an uncommonly emotional one for me. The image came to me after I had suddenly begun to feel that traditional patchwork, with its repeated symmetrical blocks, was fragmented and incomplete. My design demanded a center, a core radiating out through a progression of shapes and colors.

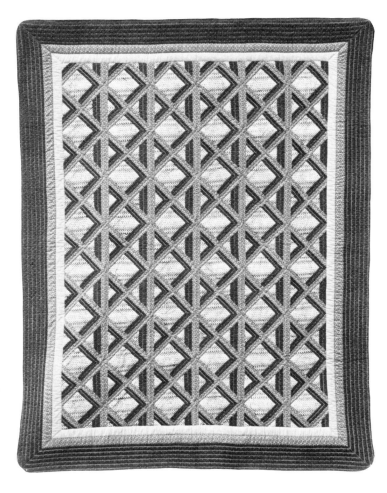

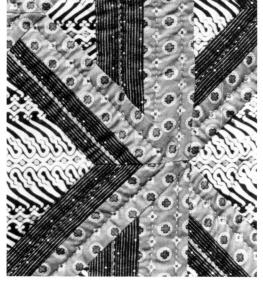

JUDY MATHIESON

Norman Wall
82 by 102 inches
1979

Cotton and an imported
Indonesian batik. Machine pieced,
hand quilted.

*This quilt was inspired by a
wallpaper pattern which I
discovered in the home of my
friends, the Normans!*

CAROLYN MULLER

Another Day
104 by 111 inches
1979

Applique, piecework. Strip pieced and quilted cotton, ribbon and trim.

My intent in this quilt was to use familiar forms that you might encounter during a typical day. Designing the quilt, I had the pleasure of playing with all the fabrics in the piece . . . typical of just "another day" in my life.

TERRIE HANCOCK MANGAT

Covington Slickers:
Rainy Days in Cincinnati
76 by 85 inches
1981

Reverse applique. Quilted by Sue Rule.

After living for three years in Oklahoma, my return to Cincinnati's wet spring seasons inspired me to make this quilt. I wanted to make a statement about a place rich in color and imagery: beautiful and oppressive at the same time.

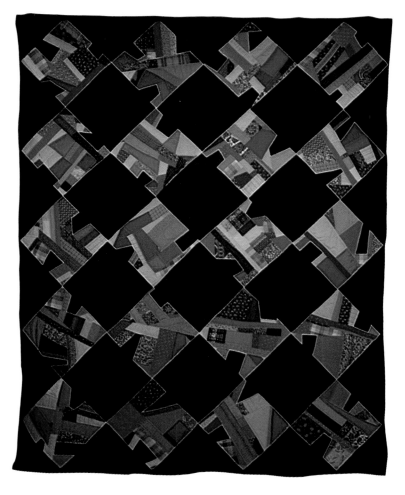

MARIE COMBS

Refractions on a Black Field
89 by 108 inches
1981

Cotton and blends. Machine pieced. Hand quilted by Anna Miller.

Until recently, I concentrated most of my energies on making quilt-like forms with stitched and layered handmade papers. Now I have moved into making real quilts, using intense, solid color combinations. All of my quilts have a narrow ¼-inch band which is inset to act as a kind of "mortar" between colors or design elements in each quilt.

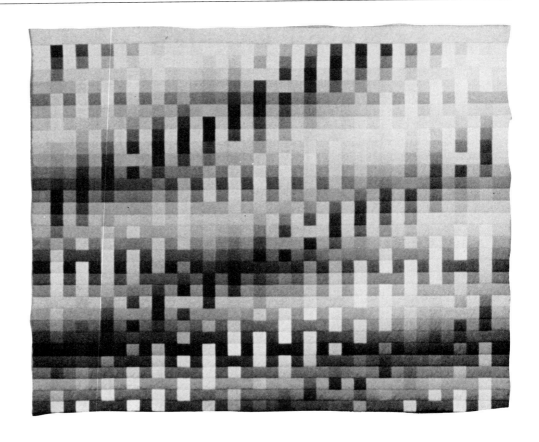

JAN MYERS

Anemone
82 by 94 inches
1981

Hand dyed cotton muslin.
Machine pieced.

*In "Anemone", I feel as though
I'm peering through a veil of steel-
blue water to the world of color
that undulates on the ocean floor.
Living in Minnesota, this is, of
course, a "national geographic"
fantasy!*

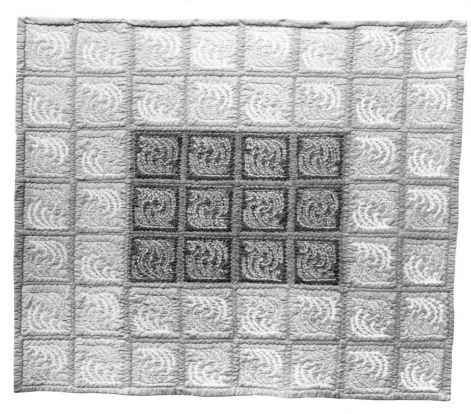

NANCY KOONS

Sea Dreams
82 by 91 inches
1979

Batiked cotton muslin. Hand
quilted.

*My move from the midwest to
Florida, my experimentation with
batik, my preference for blue and
my fascination with beaches all
culminated in "Sea Dreams."*

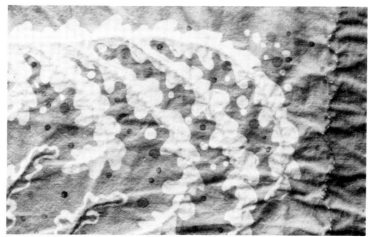

WENDA F. VON WEISE

Fabricated Landscape:
Shifted Geologic Strata
79 by 79 inches
1981

Photo-screen.

DAVID HORNUNG

Big Blue
60 by 60 inches
1981—Award of Excellence

Hand dyed cotton.

I am attracted to the object quality and graphic potential of quilts. My pieces are non-functional. My aim is to make the character of my work mirror the character of my existence.

TREVA J. IDDINGS

Necktie Dahlias
80 by 48 inches
1981

Machine appliqued ties.

ROBIN A. MCCLUSKEY

Tiger Claw
85 by 85 inches
1981

Appliqued cotton velveteen and
corduroy, silk, satin, velour.
Airbrushed. Trapunto. Photo by
Tanya A. Short.

CATHERINE JOSLYN

Pieced Quilt '80: Dreamscape
96 by 96 inches
1981

Hand dyed cotton.

SARA GILFERT

Japanese Silk Calendar Quilt:
Concealment/Revealment Series II
36 by 36 inches
1981

Handmade paper of sisal and
kozo, silk brocade and cotton
twill.

*While studying papermaking in
Japan, I collected a number of*
calendars made of washi. I tore
them in pieces and combined
them with patches of silk
brocade, handmade sisal paper
and kozo paper to create this
nine-block quilt of veiled and
partially revealed images.

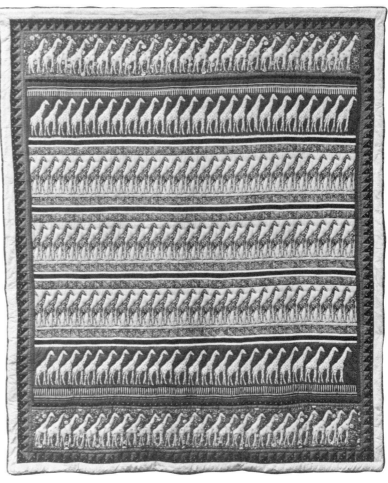

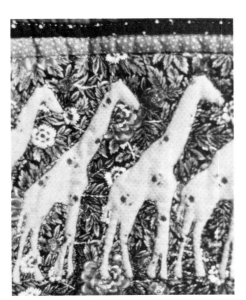

TERRIE HANCOCK MANGAT

Giraffes
86 by 96 inches
1979

Hand quilted cotton.

This piece is built around a piece of block-printed fabric which I bought in Kenya ten years ago. I used it as the center panel, the three center rows. I used a reverse applique technique to do the top and bottom two rows . . . that's over 150 giraffes! Needless to say, it took me well over a year to complete this quilt!

MARIE SHIRER

French Knot
57 by 57 inches
1981

Hand pieced and hand quilted.

"French Knot" was inspired by a stonework design on the wall of a university museum. The stones appeared to weave over and under one another, and this turned out to be a fascinating exercise in interlacing separate sections, trying to achieve the same effect.

DAVID HORNUNG

Pictorial Arrangement
60 by 72 inches
1981—Award of Excellence

Hand dyed cotton.

I dye or over-dye muslin, using a paintbrush to apply the color. I then complete the top with hand applique. I favor this process because of the design freedom it allows.

CAROL GRIBBLE

Paper Patchwork
66 by 63 inches
1981

Intaglio.

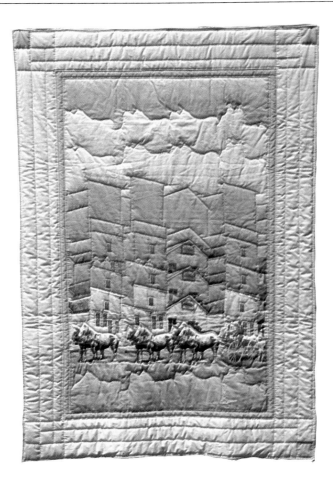

SISTER LINDA FOWLER

P. C.
98 by 67 inches
1981

Silk screened cotton.

I was particularly fond of my grandfather, P. C. Fowler, the littlest fellow on the buckboard. When he died, I wanted to make something in his memory. I enlarged an old photograph of him, taken in front of his father's business in Silverton, Colorado, and used it as a starting point for this quilt.

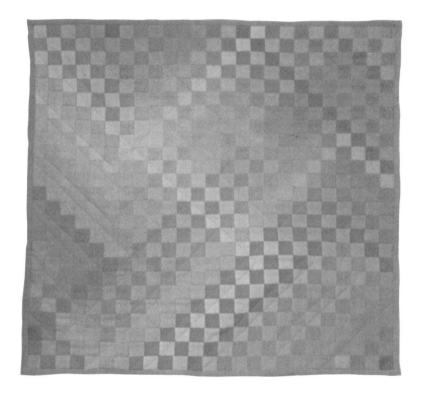

DEBRA MILLARD

Ice Flows
24 by 24 inches
1981

Hand dyed cotton, machine
pieced and hand quilted.

*Ice Flows is a study of vibrating
and vanishing boundaries
between colors. The fabrics are
hand dyed with Procion to obtain
the subtle gradations of color.
The quilt is then pieced in one-
inch squares.*

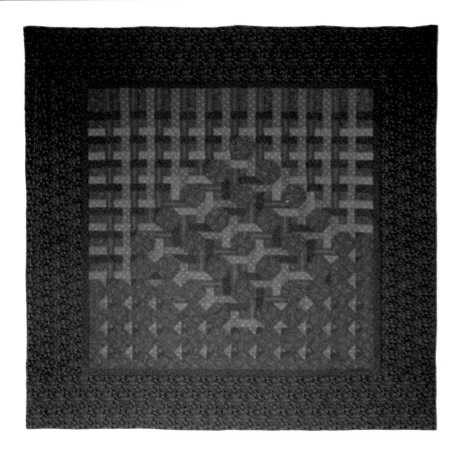

PAMELA GUSTAVSON JOHNSON

Chains and Bands
49 by 49 inches
1981

Calico and cotton.

My approach to quiltmaking is, most often, highly structured and systematic. In this quilt I chose to investigate a traditional piecing pattern by separating it into its component parts.

PATSY ALLEN

Blue Trapezium
27 by 27 inches
1981

Fabric and ribbon.

*I am interested in the theme of
spatial illusion. I start with a basic
quilt block or square, and then
disguise or de-emphasize it by
extending shapes and lines.*

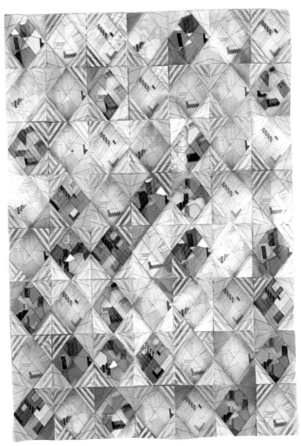

PAMELA JEAN BURG

Curtain
30 by 50 inches
1981—Best of Show

Color Xerox on acetate, with
paper, mylar and plastic thread.

This work grows from the tradition of woven textiles that are pieced and appliqued to form surfaces. The fabric is constructed of paper and plastic, incorporating both graphic patterns and subtle suggestions of intimate architectural spaces.

JUDI WARREN

Hot Möbius
68 by 68 inches
1981

Bleached, tinted and purchased
cottons. Machine pieced and hand
quilted. Photo by John Kluesener.

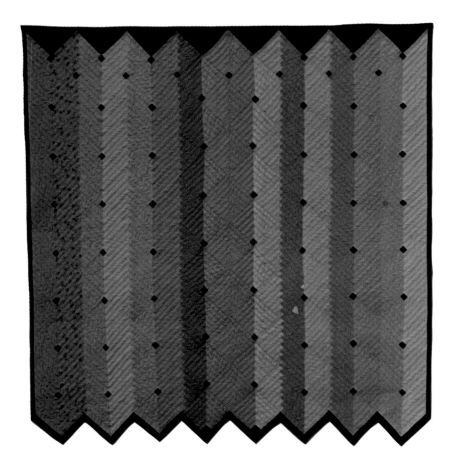

VIRGINIA RANDLES

Fences---
78 by 82 inches
1979

Cotton/polyester broadcloth.
Hand quilted by Bertha Mast.

SUZANNE KJELLAND

RainGlow
83 by 36 inches
1981

Hand dyed cotton, synthetic dyes.
Machine quilted.

YVONNE PORCELLA

A World Beyond the Clouds
72 by 48 inches
1981

Hand dyed silk.

My expertise lies in clothing of ethnic design. This Haori, a Japanese outer garment, was designed as a flat wall quilt. It can also be folded at the shoulders and tied together at the sides to form a wearable garment.

LAUREN ENGEL

Litho Quilt
61 by 61 inches
1981

Lithography on silk and cotton. Batik and hand painting with French dyes. Hand quilted.

My primary concern in quilting is image, calling for the same continuous and careful consideration that is required in painting. I have chosen the fabric medium to express images because it is more personal than painting. It invites the viewer to touch as well as look.

SUSAN KRISTOFERSON

Counting Forty-Six
26 by 48 inches
1981

Handmade paper, sewn.

MARY LOU SMITH

Williamsburg Garden
72 by 84 inches
1981

Cotton and blends.

I work with a group of friends, and we decided that each of us would make a quilt about a garden, with no further specifications. I chose a colonial door-yard garden, because I admire colonial architecture and landscaping. The precision and symmetry of this kind of garden lends itself to expression in geometric form.

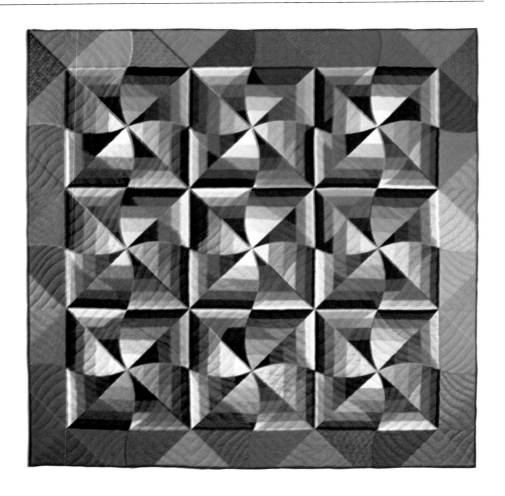

MICHAEL JAMES

Rhythmetron
68 by 68 inches
1981

Machine pieced, hand quilted
cotton.

RUTH B. MCDOWELL

Bee Balm—Monarda Didyma
40 by 40 inches
1981

Machine pieced and hand quilted
cotton.

SUSAN SHARPE

Family Photo Album
54 by 72 inches
1979

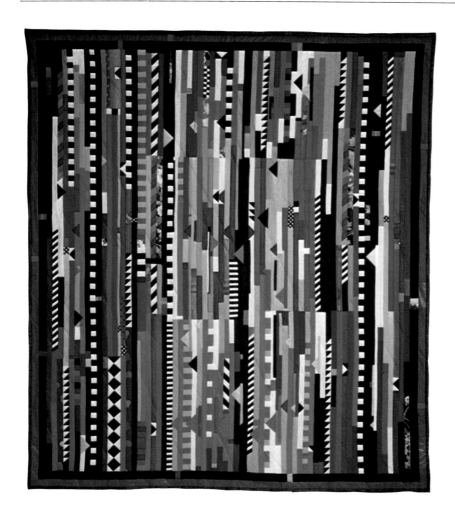

YVONNE PORCELLA

Takoage
72 by 82 inches
1981

Machine pieced and hand quilted
cotton.

ANN BIRD

Dancers
90 by 90 inches
1981

Reverse applique with cotton/
polyester.

LINDA MACDONALD

Dusk, 1981
78 by 88 inches
1981
Cotton/polyester.

RHODA COHEN

Maine Quilt
76 by 108 inches
1979

Hand pieced and hand quilted
cotton and cotton blends. Laid-on
strip and applique technique,
pieced in segments.

*This quilt was a result of
combining a very old technique
with some very new ideas of artist
Paul Klee. The quilt depicts a
landscape which is viewed from
above, below, from the side and
any other way possible.*

CHRISTINA BUCK

Medallion
54 by 54 inches
1979

Machine pieced and hand quilted
cottons and cotton blends.

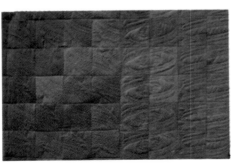

ROSALIE LAMANNA

Warm Watergate Coverup
51 by 63 inches
1979

Cotton, wool roving and wool
challis.

ESTHER PARKHURST

Four Corners
52 by 52 inches
1981

Pieced.

I "paint" my quilts piece by piece, after I've made a sketch of the design. I place individually cut pieces of fabric on an 8 by 12-foot linen-covered Cellotex wall in my studio. The linen allows the individual pieces of fabric to adhere so that I can step back and observe the overall color and design as I progress.

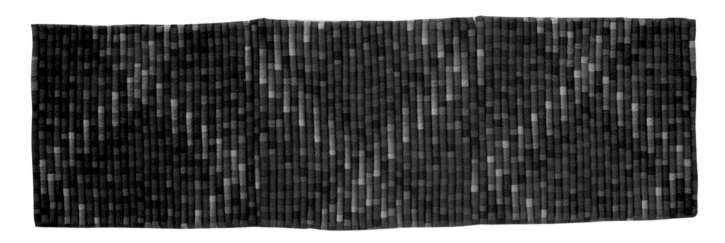

SHARLA JEAN HOSKIN

Triptych
90 by 36 inches
1979

Screen printed, channel quilted
cotton sateen. Machine quilted.

MARY JANE DEVORE

Morning Glory
72 by 80 inches
1981

Cotton and cotton/polyester.

This quilt is built around a treasured piece of fabric . . . the black floral print. I had it for at least three years before I could bear to cut into it, and then I did my best to cut it as little as possible.

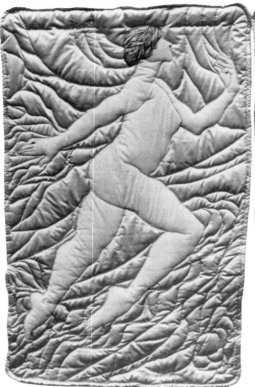 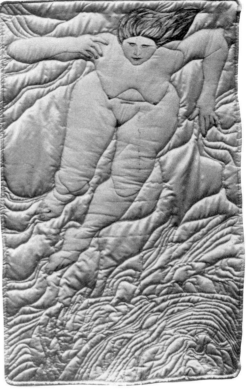

CYNTHIA NIXON-HUDSON

Floating Isadora
80 by 67 inches
1979

Muslin and satin, ink-drawn and ink-tinted. Appliqued and machine quilted.

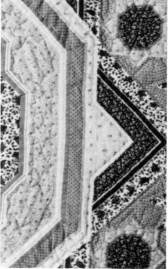

ANN BIRD

Blue Star
84 by 84 inches
1981

Cotton and cotton/polyester.
Machine pieced and hand quilted.

SHARON ROBINSON

Untitled Blanket
75 by 65 inches
1981

Dye/print, pieced quilt.

This is one in a series of horse blankets that I have made. I feel they carry on the costume tradition which has grown out of *the love and fascination that people throughout the ages have had for this beautiful and powerful animal. I love horses!*

NANCY CROW

February Study II
60 by 60 inches
1979

Cotton/polyester broadcloth.
Quilted by Velma Brill.

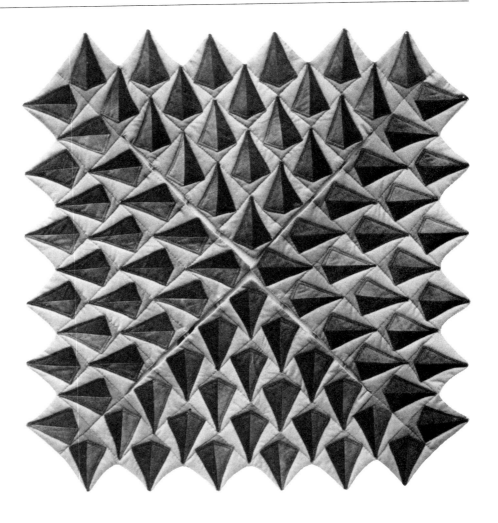

SHARON ROBINSON

Hanging Quilt IV
54 by 54 inches
1979

Dyed denim and cotton knit
fabric. Machine appliqued and
hand quilted.

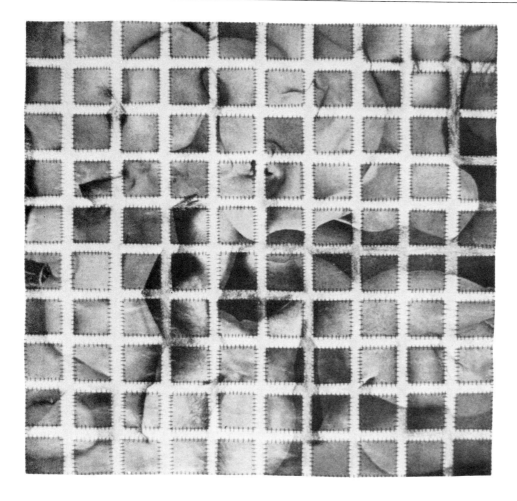

DONNA HAJZL

Paper Quilt
13 by 13 inches
1981

Paper, pencil and thread.

This quilt is one of a series in which I used paper, collage and drawn elements to create a hand sewn, quilted visual statement.

Individual collage units were placed in a grid pattern so that colors, textures and linear elements connect visually.

JUDITH LARZELERE

Marriage of Blue and Orange
76 by 108 inches
1981

Cotton. Photo by William
MacKee.

I wanted to create enormous energy, a held-in tension, with this piece so I used an orange and blue that vibrate optically. Thus, the "marriage" of blue and orange could equally and accurately be called the "conflict" of blue and orange. I will leave to the viewer the option of drawing parallels to the world of human interaction!

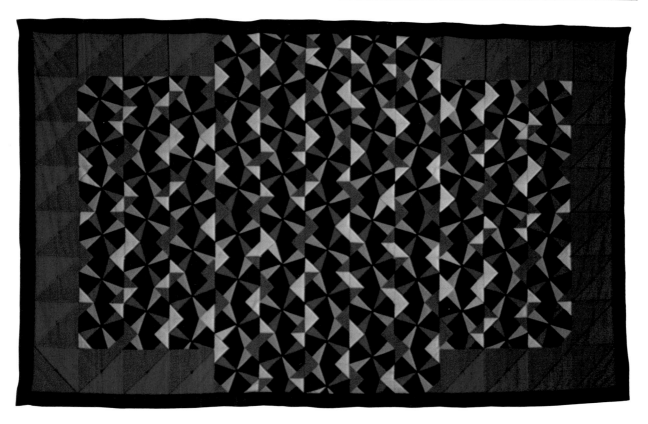

JULIE ROACH BERNER

Southwestern Festival
78 by 120 inches
1981

Quilted cotton.

FRANCOISE BARNES

Eyes of Isis
80 by 84 inches
1979

Machine pieced cottons and
cotton/polyester broadcloth. Hand
quilted by the Amish women of
Holmes County, Ohio.

PEGGY SPAETH

Boxes and Stars Quilt
72 by 72 inches.
1979

Cotton and cotton/polyester.
Machine pieced and hand quilted.

*I designed this quilt while
recovering from a broken clavicle
. . . at the same time, trying to
have a vacation in California!*

CAROLYN MULLER

Self-Portrait of a Quiltmaker
47 by 54 inches
1981

Cotton, velveteen, moire, chintz,
satin, blends and netting.

While working on this quilt, I went through a period of intense self-evaluation and questioned the validity of being a contemporary quiltmaker in today's society. I finally concluded that like so many contemporary quilt designers, I do what I do—because I must!

SUSAN KOLOJESKI MURPHY

Wrappers
36 by 45 inches
1979

Pieced, color Xerox transfers on white satin.

The gum wrappers are assembled in the traditional "Roman Stripe" pattern. I see it as a structural pun of sorts—the gum wrappers exactly fit the traditional pattern.

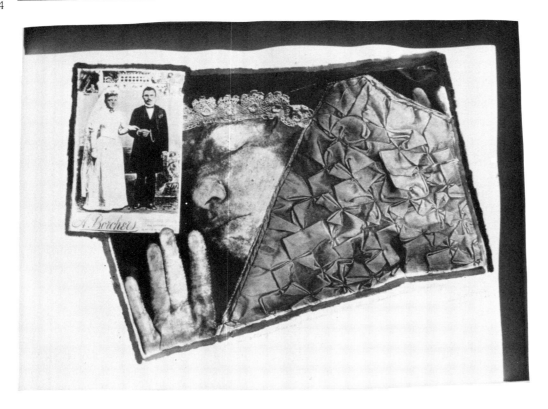

RITA DEWITT

She Had Strange Dreams
Whenever She Wore Her
Grandmother's Nightcap
12 by 16 inches
1981

Quilted paper. Hand-colored,
dimensional electrostatic collage.

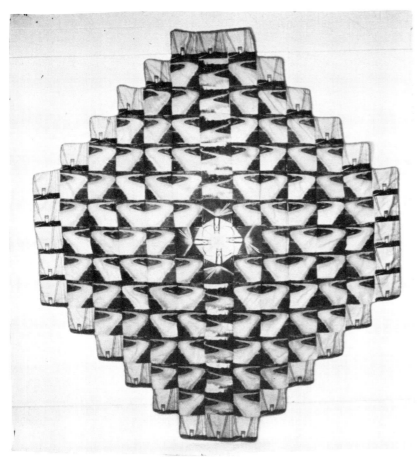

M. JOAN LINTAULT

Journey to the Mountains
110 by 110 inches
1981

Cotton strips, screened, airbrush-
dye-painted and re-woven.

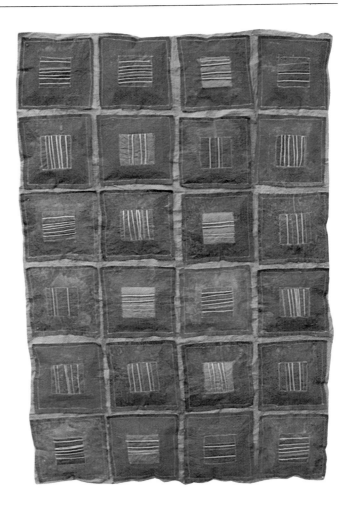

MIRJANA J. UGRINOV

Paper Quilt II
32 by 40 inches
1979

Machine quilted canvas. Brown-
bag paper with photo transfers,
ink acrylic, lace, cord and lamé.

JOY SAVILLE

Time Warp
82 by 94 inches
1981

Seminole patchwork. Photo by
John Young.

*"Time Warp" developed out of a
series of explorations I did with
the Seminole patchwork
technique. It was the "ah-ha"
stage of my efforts to create an*
*asymmetrical design which also
illustrated the illusive,
spontaneous quality I was
seeking.*

LINDA FOUTS

Family Quilt
76 by 76 inches
1981

Handmade paper, beads, canvas
and thread.

PATSY ALLEN
Nine Squares
32 by 30 inches
1981
Fabric and ribbon.

JANIE BURKE

Fruit Slices Quilt
87 by 60 inches
1981

Silk, satin and velveteen. Hand
pieced.

To get to work at Shaker Square I only pay a quarter fare.
Whether skies are gray or fair the transit system's always there.
The drivers really seem to care. Riding the Rabbit is a warm fuzzy.

JUDITH GREENE ALBERT

Rabbit Transit
56 by 36 inches
1981

Machine quilted applique, dyed
with Procion.

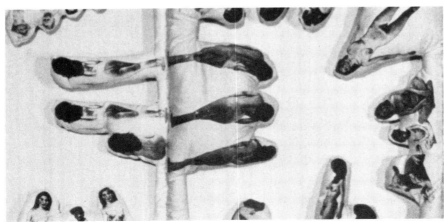

M. JOAN LINTAULT

Heavenly Bodies
56 by 64 inches
1981

*Xerox transfer on cotton/
polyester fabric. Pieced, stuffed
and quilted.*

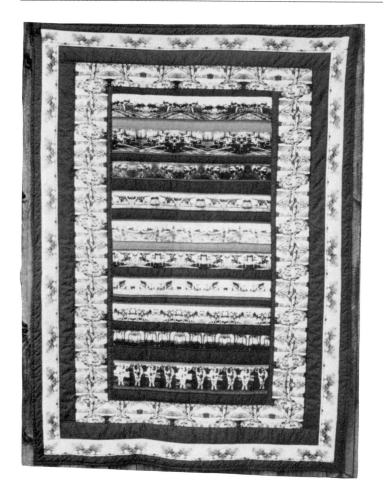

TAFI BROWN

Deer Knoll Dairy I
61 by 85 inches
1981

Cyanotype on cotton. Machine
pieced and embroidered. Hand
quilted by Margaret Bragg.

*The subjects of my quilts are
things that I love, things that
are important in my life at a
particular time.*

JEAN HEWES

The Sitter
54 by 65 inches
1981—Award for Innovative Use
of the Medium

Silk, crepe, wool, taffeta, brocade.
Appliqued and machine quilted.

I do not start out with any sketch or plan in mind for my quilts. I just begin by throwing down different fabrics on the floor, feeling how the colors and textures work together. As I continue working with the fabric, shapes and figures begin to suggest themselves.

JEAN HEWES

The Striped Lady
42 by 76 inches
1981—Award for Innovative Use
of the Medium

Cotton, linen and brocade.
Appliqued, machine and hand
quilted.

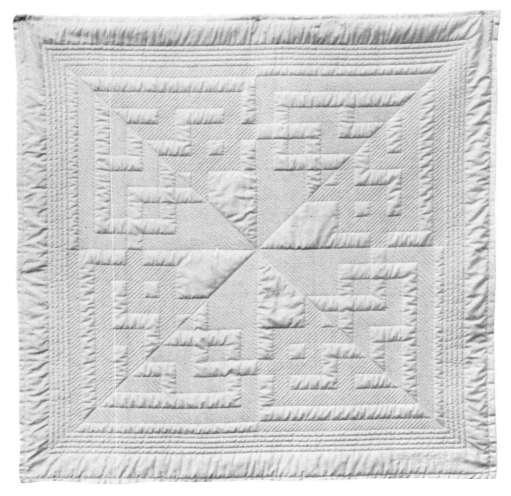

MARIA MCCORMICK-SNYDER

Labyrinth
44 by 44 inches
1979

Hand quilted polished cotton.
Whole-cloth quilt.

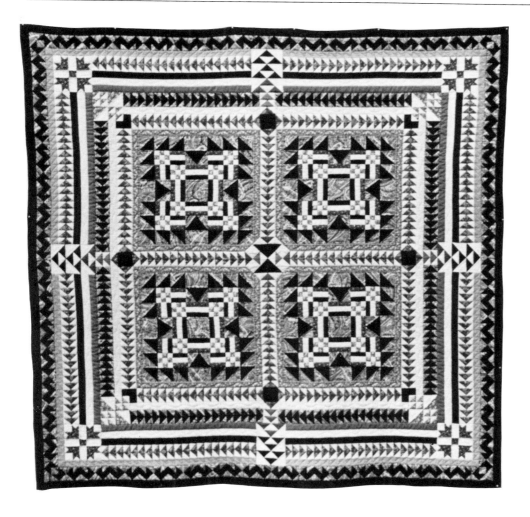

CHRIS WOLF EDMONDS

Fox and Geese
64 by 64 inches
1979

Cotton. Hand and machine
pieced, hand quilted.

*This quilt is a combination of all
the patterns I could find that had
the word "fox" or "geese" in the
title!*

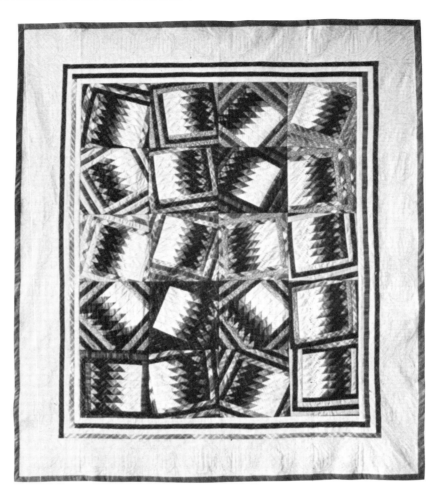

NANCY GIPPLE

Score for Bluegrass
Sewing Machine
81 by 94 inches
1981

Seminole patchwork and log cabin
piecing with shirting fabric.

*These plaid scraps were leftovers
from five shirts that I made for a
performance by the members of
my favorite Minnesota Bluegrass
band, The Armstrong Brothers
and Joan. I wanted it to be an
energetic visual song.*

SHERRY PHILLIPS

Medallion
90 by 100 inches
1979

Cotton/polyester blends and
rayon blends. Machine pieced and
hand quilted.

RUTH B. MCDOWELL

Lady's Mantle—
Alchemilla Vulgaris
40 by 40 inches
1981

Machine pieced and hand quilted
cotton.

*This is one in a series of six wall
hangings. The design is based on* *various herbs and medicinal
plants.*

JODY KLEIN

Cows Grazing Along
the Milky Way
40 by 60 inches
1979

Hand and machine quilted cotton
and cotton sateen, airbrushed and
stamped. Trapunto technique
defines the cows.

Photo by Chris Eaton.

Quilt National exhibitions are housed in this 67-year-old dairy barn in Athens, Ohio, which was saved from destruction in 1977 by a major community effort. The structure is listed on the National Register of Historic Buildings, and now accomodates a number of cultural events, sponsored by The Dairy Barn, Southeastern Ohio Cultural Arts Center, Inc.

With 7000 square feet of continuous floor space, The Dairy Barn is uniquely suited to an exhibition of quilts. The works are suspended from the ceiling and hang free of the walls, allowing the viewer to see both sides of the quilt.

Quilt National 1981
Steering Committee

Sara Gilfert, Coordinator
Pam Parker, Executive Director-
    Dairy Barn
Doreen Pallini, Exhibition Designer
Lynda Swenson, Finance
Michele Hoffman, Publicity
Porter Smith-Thayer, Programs
Pat Knable, Volunteers
Gail Good, Opening
Teri Schwindler
Kathy Andrews
Hilary Fletcher
Kit Dailey

For more information about Quilt National, or to obtain postcards or posters which feature the quilts exhibited, contact Quilt National, P.O. Box 747, Athens, Ohio 45701.

INDEX